Raves for *The Joy of Writing J*

"*The Joy of Writing Journal* invites you to get into what researchers call *flow* and keeps you fully immersed in the joyful momentum of creation. Lisa Tener has helped thousands of people break through creative blocks and develop a fulfilling writing practice. With this creative journal she will help you do that, too."

— Megan Gunnell, LMSW, Founder & Director, Thriving Well Institute

"I didn't anticipate how much *The Joy of Writing Journal* would spark my creativity. On days that it felt challenging to sit and write, the journal provided an approachable and fun access point. The lists and prompts kept me going!"

— Amber Hanks, Mindfulness Based Stress Reduction (MBSR) yoga instructor

"If you are looking for creative inspiration, writing guidance, or innovative ways to develop the effective habits of a productive writer, I can't think of a better guide than Lisa Tener. *The Joy of Writing Journal* bottles up Lisa's creative support into an easy-to-use, engaging, and fun guide that is a valuable resource whether you are journaling for personal wellbeing or using the prompts to build your muscles as a writer."

— Jon Lieff, MD, author of *The Secret Language of Cells*

"Each page of this journal contains good things that prompt you to create, learn, and evolve. Lisa inspires you to take the next step to identify and share your best self."

— Kristin Meekhof, LMSW, author of *A Widow's Guide to Healing*

"'I don't have the time' and 'I don't know what to write' are the two most common reasons people give when they are ignoring the pull to write. Lisa Tener's elegant, generous book solves both of these problems. In a simple, easy-to-follow format, she opens the door to your own garden of imagination, causing stories, ideas, and characters to spill out of you organically. The supportive, interactive 30-day structure of insightful prompts eliminates procrastination and fear. If you are looking for the writer within, look no further. This wise book is the key."

— Sam Bennett, author of *Get It Done: From Procrastination to Creative Genius in 15 Minutes a Day*

"Lisa Tener has a gift for making writing easy and fun. Each prompt in *The Joy of Writing Journal* points you to your true north. Access your joy and embrace the writing journey. Lisa's prompts and guidance helped me bring my first book into the world, and now that the floodgates are open, more books are coming!"

— Gael-Sylvia Pullen, author of *The Good Around Us*

"Writing is the way out of the pandemic malaise and Lisa Tener's *The Joy of Writing Journal* will take you to a better place."

— Cathy Turney, author of *Get 10,000+ Twitter Followers: Easily, Quickly, Ethically*

"Lisa Tener is a brilliant facilitator who helps make sitting down to write breezy and fun. *The Joy of Writing Journal* will help you slip past the gnarly gates of resistance and into the garden of words and joy."

— Tama Kieves, bestselling author of *Inspired & Unstoppable: Wildly Succeeding in Your Life's Work!*

The Joy of Writing Journal

Spark Your Creativity in 8 Minutes a Day

Expanded Edition

by Lisa Tener

Award-Winning Book Coach
and Creator of *Bring Your Book to Life*®

WORLDCHANGERS
MEDIA

Published by WorldChangers Media
PO Box 83, Foster, RI 02825
www.WorldChangers.Media

My Gifts to You

Oh, we are going to have such creative fun! But first, I have two gifts to help you on this journal journey. To receive them, hover over the digitized image with your smartphone camera on or, for an older phone, download a QR Code Reader App on your smartphone; then just scan the digitized images with your phone and your gifts will magically appear. You also may find the gifts at the links shared below.

Gift #1: Creative Manifesto

Just about every writer I know experiences some self-doubt or resistance at times. My first gift is a one-page pep talk/reminder from you to you, to help you bypass these struggles and write consistently. This one-page exercise will help you own your creativity, stop judging yourself, and enjoy the prompts of *The Joy of Writing Journal* daily.

DOWNLOAD AND PRINT:
My Creative Manifesto:
Permission to Write

https://www.lisatener.com/my-creative-manifesto

Fill out this manifesto to personalize it and use it to inspire you each day.

Gift #2: Writing in the Zone

Relaxation can help you access a state of creative flow with ease. If that appeals to you, try this short and simple meditation before writing.

LISTEN TO THE MEDITATION:
Writing in the Zone:
A Guided Journey

https://www.lisatener.com/writing-in-the-zone

Table of Contents

Foreword by Carrie Barron, MD 9

Dear Writer 11

How Writing Prompts Changed My (Writing) Life 11

The Challenges of Writers, Creatives, Visionaries, and Seekers 11

The Joy of Writing is Here for You 12

This Program is Deceptively Simple 12

My Confession about Writing Daily 13

Why 30 Days? 13

How to Get the Most out of *The Joy of Writing Journal* 13

Answers to Your Questions 14

About the Expanded Edition of *The Joy of Writing Journal* 14

What's New? 16

How to Use *The Joy of Writing Journal* 17

Week 1: Planning Page 19

Day 1: Your 5 Whys 21

Day 2: Why We Journal/Write 25

Day 3: Things That Spark Joy 29

Day 4: Writing About Place 33

Day 5: Animal Wisdom 37

Day 6: Rejuvenate Before Writing 41

Day 7: Meet Your Muse 45

Week 1: Summary 49

Week 2: Planning Page 51

Day 8: Explore Your Inner Garden 53

Day 9: An Interesting Character Enters a Scene 57

Day 10: Favorite Times to Write and Journal 61

Day 11: Permission to Be Bold 65

Day 12: Places to Visit 69

Day 13: A Stranger Knocks 73

Day 14: Visions and Dreams for My Writing Life 77

Week 2: Summary 81

Week 3: Planning Page 83
    Day 15: Enhance Your Writing Space for Creativity and Flow 85
    Day 16: My Dream Reader 89
    Day 17: Cozy Up 93
    Day 18: Inviting in Life's Magic 97
    Day 19: Move and Flow 101
    Day 20: Words We Love 105
    Day 21: How I Got Screwed Out of Inner Peace 109
    Week 3: Summary 113
Week 4: Planning Page 115
    Day 22: Perfectly Flawed 117
    Day 23: Farm to Table 121
    Day 24: An Unlikely Dialogue 125
    Day 25: Quirks as Perks 129
    Day 26: If My House Could Talk 133
    Day 27: Bless Your Little Cotton Socks 137
    Day 28: The Magic of Travel Writing 141
    Week 4: Summary 145
Future Planning Page 147
    Day 29: You Didn't Know This About Me 149
    Day 30: How to Support Your Journaling/Writing Habit 153
Time to Become a Prompts Maker! 157
    Interview You 157
    You're the Host 163
    Ask Your Muse 169
    One Curious Cookie 173
    Word Salad 177
    Word Salad #2 181
    Big Thinks 185
    Bad Habits 189
    The Good Habit 191
You Made It! 195
    Things to Do Now 195
    One More Thing 195
    Thank You! 198
Acknowledgments 199
About the Author 203
    A Favor 203
Ideas, Notes, Doodles, and Stuff 205

Foreword by Carrie Barron, MD

If anyone can spark your creativity, seed your joy, and help you cement a writing habit, it's Lisa Tener. Meeting Lisa at Harvard Medical School's publishing course changed my life. When I heard her speak, I knew I wanted to work with her.

What a great decision that was! Maybe it was her *Meet Your Muse* exercise that made me trust my intuition and crystallize my topic. Perhaps it was her capacity to hold me accountable and steer me in a direction that felt deeply right. Most of all, I think it was her empathy, encouragement, and insight that turned me from a dreamer to a doer, to begin my proposal instead of pondering it. The right kind of support from the right person can make all the difference when realizing your creative self.

More than ever, people are turning to journaling and other creative projects to conjure wellbeing and spark moments of happiness. Creativity is intrinsically rewarding. Engaging in a compelling task, from writing to crafting, makes time fall away and allows you to feel at one with yourself and the world.

The trick is establishing a process that becomes an integral part of your core being and an everyday activity. Lisa can get you there. Eight minutes a day can change your mindset, connect you to your deeper self, cement your writing habit, and cheer you up. *The Joy of Writing Journal* is a how-to journal that will turn you into a can-do writer. Lisa's deep sensitivity, vast experience, and superlative skill, distilled into this user-friendly guide, will be a tremendous support as you embark upon your writing journey.

— Carrie Barron, MD, author of *The Creativity Cure*
   Director of Creativity for Resilience, Dell Medical School

Dear Writer,

I'm so excited to share *The Joy of Writing Journal* to stimulate your imagination and happiness. *The Joy of Writing Journal* offers you these tools:

- A path for self-discovery
- A path to wellbeing
- A gift to your inner muse (that creative part of you)
- A tool to strengthen your writing practice
- A warm-up before working on bigger projects
- A way to generate new material for a blog post, short story, poem, essay, or even a book
- Or simply a way to have fun

How Writing Prompts Changed My (Writing) Life

During my senior year of college, I discovered writing prompts. They changed my life forever. Writing prompts freed me from the pressure to create from scratch by providing me with something to respond to.

Many times, my friend, Anita Killian, and I shivered on Massachusetts Avenue, in front of the entrance to MIT's Infinite Corridor waiting for the Dudley bus to Harvard Square. Once in The Square, we wound our way to the intersection of Bow and Arrow Streets to the Café Pamplona, where we worked through the prompts in Natalie Goldberg's *Writing Down the Bones* and drank the best hot chocolate west of Salzburg, Austria. Surrounded by philosophical conversations typical of college and graduate students, we felt a part of something bigger than us—community.

The Challenges of Writers, Creatives, Visionaries, and Seekers

In my over two dozen years of working with—and teaching—thousands of writers and creatives, I have found these are their biggest challenges:

- Developing self-confidence
- Discovering discipline/consistency of writing
- Getting into a state of flow
- Overcoming resistance
- Writing from an inspired state to create their best work
- Completing projects, not just starting them

The Joy of Writing is Here for You

The Joy of Writing Journal is designed to recreate both the stimulus and freedom of playful prompts and the sense of community Anita and I felt in cozy Café Pamplona. Throughout this journal you'll find QR codes (the computer-generated squares) to scan with your smartphone, which will connect you to a message from me or a response to these prompts from other writers across the nation and the world. And you can respond to these videos with your own. In this way, I hope you feel welcomed by, and connected to, a vast community of journalers, writers, poets, bloggers, journalists, and authors—some who are highly accomplished and some who are new to the discipline of writing.

The purpose of *The Joy of Writing Journal* is to help you write, write, write; to make it easy for you to be creative; and to allow you to let go of any worrying you may do over writing perfectly or writing for an audience. Write for you. Let *The Joy of Writing Journal* help you remember and experience the joy of writing daily as it assists you with any or all of the six challenges mentioned earlier.

The prompts in this journal support you to hone your craft as well as your writing habit. They focus on a wide variety of topics for different purposes:

- Prompts about people help you weave their personalities and quirks into interesting characters, whether they become the stuff of fiction, memoir, poetry, essay, a blog post, a screenplay, or an inspiring anecdote in a self-help or how-to book.
- Prompts that ask about experiences and places assist you in telling both nonfiction and fictional stories, developing both plot and setting.
- Other prompts help you write with depth, honesty, and vulnerability.
- Some encourage you to develop comfort and facility with dialog.
- Some inspire insights about your personality and life journey.

As you respond to the prompts, you may be tempted to judge some of your writing as boring or stupid. Don't judge; just write. Not everything needs to be a work of art. Practice is enough.

This Program is Deceptively Simple

It may seem as if there isn't much to this program: setting a planned time to write, making a list, exploring a daily prompt, and watching an optional supplementary video or audio to inspire you and help you know you belong to this vast, supportive community of writers—some aspiring, some published, and some bestsellers. In fact, the power of the program is in its simplicity.

The Joy of Writing Journal will get you into the practice of writing. There's nothing easier to write than a list; so, most days, we start there: with a list. Then you continue to write by choosing one thing from the list to write about. Sometimes the prompt will be obvious and other days you might be surprised by what I ask you to do with your list. You're already writing once you make a list, so it's a snap to take the next baby step into exploring and expounding.

My Confession about Writing Daily

I must admit that I do not always write daily. Sometimes I do, and create some of my best work, experiencing the thrill of heightened creativity. These sustained periods of daily writing have helped me complete projects and hone my craft. But I've learned that it's okay to experience fallow periods, too. I see these as times to refresh and prepare for my next big writing project. However, during the 30 days of using this journal, I encourage you to write daily. If you do miss a day, no judgment; just pick up where you left off.

Why 30 Days?

Research shows that it takes 21 days or more to create a habit. By Day 21, you can consider yourself a consistent writer and be confident in your ability to generate new material. Here's more:

- Extensive research shows that journaling daily supports wellbeing and happiness.
- Writing daily helps you practice and polish your writing skills.
- Daily writing enables you to get into a state of inspiration and flow more easily. Even if down the road you write less frequently, your ability to tap into flow will likely remain easier to access.
- Writing daily gives you confidence as a writer.
- Consistent writing helps you to complete projects. Completed projects means you can publish, reach readers, make an impact, and move on to the next project with a sense of accomplishment.

So, can you commit to 30 days of writing? Try it!

How to Get the Most out of *The Joy of Writing Journal*

While this program is fairly self-explanatory, here are a few tips:

Tip #1: Use the weekly pages to commit to specific times each day when you'll write in the journal. Decide how often you'll journal. If you respond to one prompt a day, you will fill the entire journal in a month and will know yourself to be a writer who can write daily.

Tip #2: Keep the journal in a place you'll see each day to help you stick to your commitment. How about your bedside table so you can write in it morning, evening, or both?

Tip #3: Keep your phone handy to scan the codes, but put it on airplane mode when you're not using it to access *The Joy of Writing Journal* videos, audio meditations, or PDFs. Your phone will be a tool for greater engagement, but only if it doesn't distract you.

Tip #4: Go Wild: Yes, there are lines for writing, but feel free to doodle—or not. Did I mention there are no hard and fast rules?

Answers to Your Questions

Question #1: Do I have to list the exact number of items in a list?

Great question. You don't have to, but I do encourage you to do so. I purposely chose some lists to be longer, because the items at the end of the list tend to force you to go deeper or wilder or bolder. Try it!

Question #2: What happens after 30 days?

I'm glad you asked. Okay, truthfully, I'm glad I asked, but maybe you're wondering, too. One wonderful thing about *The Joy of Writing* program is that by the time you've finished, you've created lists of multiple topics and generally chosen just one or two topics to work with each day. After you complete the 30 days, you can go back and choose another, and another. *The Joy of Writing Journal* is designed to provide inspiration for many more months of writing.

About the Expanded Edition of *The Joy of Writing Journal*

Publishing a book is always an act of trust, faith, and surrender—trust that the book will find its readers or its readers will find the book, faith that the book will have a positive impact, and surrender to the ways it will happen.

Of course, as an author, you can come up with a plan for reaching specific groups of readers, but part of the magic of being an author is serving as witness to what happens when that book comes into the world.

When I wrote *The Joy of Writing Journal*, here's who I imagined I wrote for:

- Young women like the "me" in my early twenties—looking for inspiration as I scribbled away in a coffeehouse. Books like *Writing Down the Bones* led me from self-doubt to a state of flow, and I envisioned a book that would do that for the next generations of young writers.

- Journal-enthusiasts and others who, like me in my thirties, might be in a burnout job or sick with a mysterious illness (or both) and seeking answers through journaling—what's the source of this? How do I heal? What choices do I have? How can I find a joyful life again?

- Or people looking to make journaling a consistent habit. They know this habit can have a powerful effect on their lives but they struggle with a daily practice. Once established, this simple practice provides them with deep healing, personal growth, healthy relationships, and fulfillment beyond what they even dreamed of. Journaling provides them insights into the person they were and the person they are becoming—or rediscovering. Journaling helps them realize their dreams.

- Writers, like me in my fifties, looking to find consistent support to easily start their morning with writing—a journal practice that easily flows into working on bigger projects, like books; a practice that leads to both prolific work and experiencing the high—or bliss—of writing in a state of flow.

- Wise ones who know it's time to share their deep wisdom and their colorful stories but they're just not sure of the way in to creative writing.

Lo and behold, readers came and some looked like all the me's I've described for you, but many looked quite different:

- A mom wrote to tell me that she and her eight-year-old-son, who suffers from anxiety, were using *The Joy of Writing Journal* in the evenings—reading the short notes and using the prompts to write. The practice eased his anxiety, fueled his creativity, and brought them together in an intimate, shared activity.

- Three male podcasters told me they used *The Joy of Writing Journal* to generate ideas for their podcasts. Another podcaster, Kate Hanley, tried my Meet Your Muse meditation, which you'll find on Day 7, on her wonderful podcast *How to Be a Better Person*. As I led her through the practice, her muse, a female gnome who lived in a tree house, offered her a plate of cookies and the idea that she had plenty of ideas to choose from. While the muse gave her more of a "trust yourself" message than specific ideas, the post-interview conversation led to a cascade of ideas and possible guests—just as the muse had promised with the plate of cookies.

- Several entrepreneurs told me they used the journal to generate more authentic, aligned writing for their marketing activities—to more deeply connect with clients and potential customers, in a way that felt genuine—a true expression of their brand.

- Another friend told me she used *The Joy of Writing Journal* for the first project in homeschooling her niece. They, too, worked through the prompts together.

So, who are you and how will you use this journal? I'd love to know!

You can work through this journal on your own, perhaps when you first wake up in the morning, or you can gather a group of friends to write together and share—or not share—your writing. Writing in community is a powerful practice, greater than the sum of its parts. You can share this book with other adults, kids, family members, friends—it works well in community. But you can just as easily use it privately and find a sense of support through the accompanying videos and audios. You can even join other journalers and writers in our Facebook group.

What's New?

Since publishing *The Joy of Writing Journal* in September of 2021, the book has gone on to win two major book awards—the 2022 Nautilus Book Award and the 2022 Independent Publisher Book Award. All of the content that made the journal an award-winning book is here in this expanded edition.

One of my goals in writing is always to give readers potent experiences and tools they can use for their creative process—for the rest of their lives. I designed the prompts in ways that you can continue to use them for well over 30 days—many hundreds.

In this expanded edition, I also teach you to fish for yourself. After working through the 30 days of prompts, you will learn to create your own prompts—and then answer them. In this way, you can create your own journals—for yourself or even for other readers. I hope and trust that this new tool will lead to even more fulfilling exploration.

In fact, after creating the new "create your prompts" section, and having beta readers test them and provide feedback, I tried the exercises on myself. I was amazed how using these new prompts and prompts-making tools took my writing to a whole new level. I hope it will do the same for you.

How to Use *The Joy of Writing Journal*

Get comfy: Curl up in a cozy spot—your bed, a sumptuous loveseat, a sunny lounge on your deck, or at a table at an outdoor café—with this journal, a favorite pen, and your phone. What? My phone? Yes, I have some delightful treats—videos, audio meditations, and other goodies—you can access by a quick hover and click with your phone camera.

To use this journal to its full potential, I recommend responding to one prompt per day for 30 days, completing them in the order they appear. And don't forget, this interactive journal also includes optional videos and audios to enhance your experience. As mentioned, you can scan the QR codes (the computer-generated squares) with a smartphone to watch videos, listen to meditations, or download PDFs to enrich your experience as part of our journaling and writing community. All you need to do is open the camera on your phone and hover over the square QR code. Your phone camera will prompt you with, "Tap here to go to..." Just tap to see the video and tap again to play it!

In some videos, I'll be your coach, mentor, and guide, providing tips and encouragement. In other videos, I'll share my own quirky reactions to a few of the prompts. You'll also hear stories, guided visualizations, and favorite writing inspirations. You'll meet other journalers and writers—novices, new authors, and even a few bestselling authors. You'll be introduced to writers I coached to write and publish exceptional books. And you'll hear from my colleagues, mentors, and author crushes.

If you are reading this journal as an ebook, simply click on the links I've provided to access the videos, audios, and PDFs.

If you haven't yet received my special gifts to you—Gift #1: Creative Manifesto and Gift #2: Writing in the Zone—flip back to the beginning of this journal and download them now. I think you'll find them to be helpful and inspirational.

Also, feel free to join my private Facebook group: Write and Create with Lisa Tener. There, you'll find support, community, inspiration, and accountability to cultivate creative flow and get your wonderful writing done.

JOIN THE FACEBOOK GROUP:
Write and Create with Lisa Tener

https://www.facebook.com/groups/writeandcreatewithlisatener

And now … Welcome to *The Joy of Writing Journal.* This video will provide you with a few words of welcome, encouragement, and inspiration.

WATCH THE VIDEO:
Welcome to *The Joy of Writing Journal*

https://www.lisatener.com/welcome-to-the-joy-of-writing-journal/

Week 1: Planning Page

Days and Times I'll Write

Write in the date and time you plan to write. Once you complete a prompt, return here and color in the dot.

Day 1: Date _____ Time for Writing: _____ Prompt completed: ○

Day 2: Date _____ Time for Writing: _____ Prompt completed: ○

Day 3: Date _____ Time for Writing: _____ Prompt completed: ○

Day 4: Date _____ Time for Writing: _____ Prompt completed: ○

Day 5: Date _____ Time for Writing: _____ Prompt completed: ○

Day 6: Date _____ Time for Writing: _____ Prompt completed: ○

Day 7: Date _____ Time for Writing: _____ Prompt completed: ○

Plan for at least 8 minutes to make your list, do the journaling exercise, and, optionally, scan/watch the short video (or listen to the audio meditation). If you're on a roll, by all means write for as long as you want.

Day 1
Your 5 Whys

Most days, we begin by making a list, then choosing one or more items on the list to apply to the prompt. In today's video, you'll learn why this method works to get you writing in the zone! Open the camera on your smartphone and hover it over the square QR code. Your phone camera will prompt you with, "Tap here to go to..." Just tap to see the video and tap again to play it!

WATCH THE VIDEO:

What's With the Lists?

https://www.lisatener.com/whats-with-the-lists/

Writing prompts have stimulated some of the most creative periods in my writing life. I woke up one morning inspired to write this book to help other writers access the flow and productivity I experience in my most creative periods.

Let's start with why you picked up *The Joy of Writing Journal.*

List five reasons you bought (or picked up) this book:

1. _____
2. _____
3. _____
4. _____
5. _____

Pick one and explore it. What prompted you to open or buy this journal? Are you interested in the health and mood-boosting benefits of journaling? Do you want to explore your creativity? Are you looking for inspiration for a writing project? What do you hope to gain by buying and using this book?

"I journal to know what I think and feel, to expand my perceptions. Writing often carries me to a new place of understanding."

— Lisa Tener

"Finding your way does not always require doing it alone."

— Gael-Sylvia Pullen, *The Good Around Us*

Day 2
Why We Journal/Write

Why do we write? I asked published authors, aspiring authors, bloggers, and people from all walks of life why they write. Here's what they said and, in one case, sang!

WATCH THE VIDEO:
Why We Journal or Write

https://www.lisatener.com/why-we-journal-or-write/

Writing often leaves me feeling uplifted. How about you?

List five things journaling or writing does for you (or you hope it will do):

1. _____
2. _____
3. _____
4. _____
5. _____

Explore one or more of these benefits of journaling and writing. For example, how does journaling, at its best, make you feel? What happens inside you? Write about an instance where your writing had an impact on you or someone who read your writing. What happened?

"Journaling helps us grow. Creativity uplifts. Writing helps us know we're alive—truly, fully present."

— Lisa Tener

"Without some form of creative action, it is hard to feel content."

— Dr. Carrie Barron, *The Creativity Cure*

Day 3
Things That Spark Joy

Watch the video to see what sparks joy for some of the writers I know:

WATCH THE VIDEO:
Things That Spark Joy

https://www.lisatener.com/things-that-spark-joy/

    In addition to writing, climbing the rocks along the opening to Narragansett Bay fills me with joy. Whether I'm experiencing a bright afternoon with the sun reflecting off the mica embedded in the granite, or a misty morning with the white quartz crystals giving off an otherworldly glow, my time in nature often nourishes my writing.

Name ten things that spark joy for you.

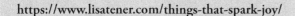

1. _____
2. _____
3. _____
4. _____
5. _____
6. _____
7. _____
8. _____
9. _____
10. _____

Pick one and do it; then write about it.

"Listen to the wind and birds. Now, the trees. When you can hear the grass, you'll know you're truly listening."

— Lisa Tener

"I am all for people writing out of the sheer joy of it."

— Ginger Moran, author of *The Algebra of Snow*

Day 4
Writing About Place

Watch the video for three tips to help you write about place in a way that deeply engages a reader (or yourself) in the experience:

WATCH THE VIDEO:

Tips for Writing About Place

https://www.lisatener.com/tips-for-writing-about-a-place/

I love writing on the dock by the Saugatucket River near my home, alone or with a friend. The denizens of the river—dragonflies, damselflies, a heron, the painted turtles, and an occasional snapping turtle—inspire poetry and open the gateways to longer projects that bubble beneath the surface.

List five places where you love to write:

1.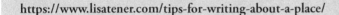
2.
3.
4.
5.

Pick one you can go to right now and write. Write about your favorite writing place, or an experience in that setting.

"I created a little nook in a room of my own and that's where I love to write. My mother's chaise is nestled in the bay windows and when the light is streaming in, it's my own slice of perfection."

— Robin Kall, host and creator of *Reading with Robin*

"Fresh air and good breathing revive the body and mind."

— Mara M. Zimmerman, *How to Meditate and Why*

Day 5
Animal Wisdom

Watch the video for a story of a recent dream of mine where animals showed up with interesting superpowers:

WATCH THE VIDEO:

The Wisdom and Play of Animals

https://www.lisatener.com/the-wisdom-and-play-of-animals

 As a kid, I felt both afraid of—and fascinated by—most wild animals. Some of them were big, like the bears at the neighborhood dump outside Fundy National Park in New Brunswick, Canada, which we viewed from the safety of our Mercury Marquis. And some were small, such as the occasional spider in my bedroom. But no matter their size, I spent many hours enthralled, just watching them. As an adult, I've come to realize that animals have so much to teach us as we observe them, connect with them, dream about them, and communicate.

List five animals you love or fear, or love to fear.

1. _____
2. _____
3. _____
4. _____
5. _____

 Pick one and let it tell a story or share its wisdom teachings. Or pick two and imagine a dialogue between them. Or combine several of them into a mythical creature and describe it.

_____

_____

_____

_____

_____

_____

_____

_____

_____

_____

_____

_____

_____

_____

_____

_____

"But especially he loved to run in the dim twilight of the summer midnights, listening to the subdued and sleepy murmurs of the forest, reading signs and sounds as a man may read a book, and seeking for the mysterious something that called—called, waking or sleeping, at all times, for him to come."

— Jack London, *The Call of the Wild*

"The more we learn about life from nature's perspective, the less
sure we can be about absolute reality."

— Kari Hohne, from the *Live Green and Blossom* course

Day 6
Rejuvenate Before Writing

In this video, I share three of my favorite ways to rejuvenate before writing in order to put forth your most inspired work:

WATCH THE VIDEO:

Ways to Rejuvenate Before Writing

https://www.lisatener.com/ways-to-rejuvenate-before-writing/

When I feel spent and too tired to write, I wander my yard or hike to the beach and woods. Practicing qigong (similar to yoga or tai chi) underneath the weeping cherry tree or on my favorite path in the woods revives me and restores my creative passion. When you come to your writing burned out, it's hard to tap your genius. When you rejuvenate, creativity flows.

List five things you can do to rejuvenate before writing:

1. _____
2. _____
3. _____
4. _____
5. _____

Now, pick one and do it. Then write about the experience.

"Be generous with your muse. Come to her refreshed and revitalized, with
love and gratitude in your heart, and she will be generous with you."

— Lisa Tener

"There's nothing like a little music to get the creative juices flowing."
— Bryan Hutchinson, *The First Draft is Not Crap*

Day 7
Meet Your Muse

In one of my favorite ways to coach writers, I lead them through a guided visualization or meditation to connect them with their creative inner source for guidance. I call this exercise "Meet Your Muse." In this inner journey, we bring our questions and challenges, and ask the inner muse for clarity, insights, ideas, and even an inner shift. The muse loves to show up creatively. My clients have introduced me to muses that include wise beings, angels, a mouse, a jester, the ocean, light, a religious figure, a version of themselves, a chain-smoking homeless woman, and a golden Buddha. Sometimes the muse shows up as a deep sense of knowing or an inner voice without any symbolism.

Let's see how it shows up for you today.

This guided meditation will help you connect to your muse:

LISTEN TO THE MEDITATION:

Meet Your Muse

https://www.lisatener.com/meet-your-muse-4/

My inner muse is _____.

Describe your muse and write about it/him/her/them.

"The creative muse loves to play. Playfulness is liberating. It helps us go beyond linear thinking and make creative connections we didn't see before."

— Lisa Tener

"Then get moving. Dance, yell, run in circles—whatever shows the world your excitement and passion. Be an exclamation point!"

— Nina Amir, *Creative Visualization for Writers*

Week 1: Summary

Congratulations! You've finished a full week of prompts.

Connect on the Facebook Group

Feel free to join us on the Facebook group and share your insights or post a video of yourself reading a paragraph or two of something you wrote using this journal.

VISIT AND/OR JOIN THE FACEBOOK GROUP:
Write and Create with Lisa Tener

https://www.facebook.com/groups/writeandcreatewithlisatener

Week 1: Inspiration

Things that happened this week that I could write about:

1. _____

2. _____

3. _____

4. _____

5. _____

Things that inspired me this week:

1. _____

_____

2. _____

_____

3. _____

_____

4. _____

_____

5. _____

_____

Be sure to color in the "prompts completed" circles from the beginning of Week 1 and give yourself a pat on the back. Well done.

Week 2: Planning Page

Welcome to Week 2!

Write in the day and time you plan to write. Once you complete a prompt, return here and color in the dot.

Day 8: Date _____ Time for Writing: _____ Prompt completed: ○

Day 9: Date _____ Time for Writing: _____ Prompt completed: ○

Day 10: Date _____ Time for Writing: _____ Prompt completed: ○

Day 11: Date _____ Time for Writing: _____ Prompt completed: ○

Day 12: Date _____ Time for Writing: _____ Prompt completed: ○

Day 13: Date _____ Time for Writing: _____ Prompt completed: ○

Day 14: Date _____ Time for Writing: _____ Prompt completed: ○

Plan for at least 8 minutes to make your list, do the journaling exercise, and, optionally, scan/watch the short video (or listen to the audio meditation). If you're on a roll, by all means write for as long as you want.

Day 8

Explore Your Inner Garden

Imagine transporting yourself to a paradise-like garden where nature nourishes you as you write in a state of deep creative flow. Wouldn't it be powerful to access an inner landscape like this no matter where you write?

Listen to this guided visualization to experience your secret inner garden—or just imagine your inner garden by reading the text below:

LISTEN TO THE MEDITATION:

Explore Your Inner Garden

https://www.lisatener.com/explore-your-inner-garden/

Close your eyes and imagine walking up a path to a secret garden. Imagine that you open a gate and enter a space where you are surrounded by beauty, with many varied landscapes and areas to be and create.

Write about the path, the gate, the garden. Employ all your senses. Explore.

_____

_____

_____

_____

_____

_____

_____

_____

_____

_____

_____

_____

_____

_____

_____

"Return to the mind that is restful and curious, perched just beyond the outskirts of the universe."

— Kari Hohne, from the *Live Green and Blossom* course

_____

_____

_____

_____

_____

_____

_____

_____

_____

_____

_____

_____

_____

_____

_____

_____

Using Your Inner Garden for Inspiration

Watch this video to discover how you can use your inner garden for writing and journaling inspiration:

> **WATCH THE VIDEO:**
>
> Using Your Inner Garden for Inspiration
>
> https://www.lisatener.com/using-your-inner-garden-for-inspiration/

Day 9
An Interesting Character Enters a Scene

Watch the video to hear about a lesson I learned in second grade, one that helped me write about people I know:

WATCH THE VIDEO:

What I Learned About Character in Second Grade

https://www.lisatener.com/what-i-learned-about-character-in-second-grade/

My mother-in-law is one of the most entertaining people I know. Rules don't apply to her and she'll do things I would never dare—like sneak into a yoga retreat that's full. Just being around her has made me a little more daring. If I were asked to list her personality traits, I would include entertaining and daring.

Now it's your turn to think about interesting character traits you could use for a character you are writing about.

Ten interesting personality traits, some you might consider flaws, others quirky, and others strengths:

1. _____

2. _____

3. _____

4. _____

5. _____

6. _____

7. _____

8. _____

9. _____

10. _____

Pick one or more of these traits and create a character, or think of a person with these traits. Imagine that character/person in a suspenseful or high-stakes scene. What happens?

_____

_____

_____

_____

_____

_____

_____

_____

_____

_____

_____

_____

_____

"I love insecure characters because they seem real to me."

— Frances Caballo, author of *Social Media Just for Writers*

"I'm not paying to have my head shrunk. I'm so interesting they ought to pay me."

— Ruth Harris, *Decades*

Day 10
Favorite Times to Write and Journal

In this video, several writers share their thoughts on their favorite times to write:

WATCH THE VIDEO:

Favorite Times to Write and Journal

https://www.lisatener.com/favorite-times-to-write-and-journal/

I love to write first thing in the morning while my inner critic still slumbers and I enjoy easy access to that dreamy, twilight state. How about you?

My favorite time to write, journal, or be creative is: _____ .

Write about why. What's magical or effective about that hour/time? Write about an experience of writing during that optimal time.

"Journal in the morning and start the day off with a little
inspiration and magic."

— Lisa Tener

"My favorite time to write is in the late evenings/early mornings, when the rest of the world (and my family) is asleep and I can concentrate on my characters. At those times, I enter the world of my book, look around, and write about what I see, feel, and experience."

— Lynne Heinzmann, author of *Frozen Voices*

Day 11
Permission to Be Bold

This video reveals what some of my students and colleagues would write about if they were a hundred times bolder:

WATCH THE VIDEO:

Permission to Be Bold

https://www.lisatener.com/permission-to-be-bold/

Sometimes, I imagine I hear my ancestors knocking on the door asking me to tell their stories. In her youth, my Grandma Stella immigrated to New York from the Russian Pale (though she insisted she was born in Connecticut, where I'm not even sure she ever set foot). Stella sang in nightclubs from her teens and into her seventies and the intense emotion in her singing made me uncomfortable. My Grandma Lily shared stories of growing up in Vienna: the manor farm her uncle managed where her mother sent her to "fatten up" and where she learned to love animals; the ballroom dancing lessons with her cousins; music nights in Vienna where the young people gathered in her home, playing their instruments and singing songs late into the night, and then spilling into the cafes in the wee hours of the morning. Up to now, I have not been able to find the courage to write about any of my ancestors. I'm afraid I won't do their stories justice and, truthfully, the journey scares me, too. What secrets might I uncover about my family's past? A hundred times bolder, maybe I'd just dive in.

Your turn.

List five things you might write about if you were a hundred times bolder:

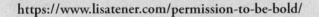

1. _____

2. _____

3. _____

4. _____

5. _____

Pick one and explore. Go bold. Get a little crazy! You have permission!

"Writing bold is less about big and more about deep. Ask yourself the same question again and again until you write an answer that surprises you."

— Lisa Tener

"I'm stepping out of the shadows into your bright, loving, all-seeing light."

— Samantha Bennett, *Start Right Where You Are*

Day 12
Places to Visit

In this video, I share about an adventure I had teaching and traveling in Bangkok:

WATCH THE VIDEO:
Traveler's Dream

https://www.lisatener.com/travelers-dream/

My parents once took my brother, sister, and me on a rare excursion to a Thai restaurant in Manhattan where I saw a poster of a Thai Buddhist temple. From then on, I dreamed of visiting that exotic land. Forty years later, I got the chance when a client invited me to teach a short version of my *Bring Your Book to Life* program in Bangkok. I wrote in my journal throughout the journey, and I plan, one day, to turn those notes into a short book.

Does travel stimulate your writing?

Ten places I've always wanted to visit:

1. _____

2. _____

3. _____

4. _____

5. _____

6. _____

7. _____

8. _____

9. _____

10. _____

Pick one. What do you know about that place? What do you imagine about it? Why do you want to visit? Imagine a visit there and write about it.

"When you travel afar and the scents and sounds of the local flora and fauna lull you to sleep and then show up in your dreams, you know you've arrived."

— Lisa Tener

"Traveling often offers a chance to say 'Yes!' to the unexpected invitation, something you'd never do at home. And when you experience the unknown, you step into the real magic of a place and its inhabitants."

— Lisa Tener

Day 13
A Stranger Knocks

In this video, you can hear first lines that some of our favorite authors came up with for the exercise that follows:

WATCH THE VIDEO:
A Stranger Knocks

https://www.lisatener.com/a-stranger-knocks/

In college, I studied with playwright A. R. "Pete" Gurney, Jr. In one of his classes, I wrote a scene inspired by an old traditional English ballad, "Get Up and Bar the Door." The ballad inspires today's prompt as well.

"A stranger knocks on my door…" What happens next? List five possibilities.

1. _____

2. _____

3. _____

4. _____

5. _____

Pick one and have fun creating an adventure tale, or a one-page thriller, or a love letter, or whatever your imagination conjures.

"The point of this task is not to finish but to start; don't worry about how it will end."

— Dawn Montefusco, poet and book coach

"[Journaling] helps me sort the wisdom from the noise."

— Stephanie Hrehirchuk, author of
An Accidental Awakening

Day 14
Visions and Dreams for My Writing Life

This video reveals the dreams of writers we love:

WATCH THE VIDEO:
Visions and Dreams of Writers We Love

https://www.lisatener.com/visions-and-dreams-of-writers-we-love/

After publishing my first book, it took me over a decade to finally finish another. Striving for perfection, we can stifle our dreams. Many of my wild or not-so-wild visions include writing in multiple genres—a book of poems, a novel, a playful little book about teaching writing in Bangkok.

Five wild visions or dreams for your writing and life are:

1. _____

2. _____

3. _____

4. _____

5. _____

Pick one and imagine this dream or vision coming true. Or, even bolder, live out the dream and then write about it!

"I have a story, a message, and I want to write it down. Thus begins your journey toward self-realization through the written word!"

— Gabriella Gafni, writer and ghostwriter

"Your limited story applies only to your limited self."

— Tama Kieves, *Inspired and Unstoppable:*
Wildly Succeeding in Your Life's Work!

Week 2: Summary

Wow! You've finished two full weeks of prompts. Give yourself a huge pat on the back.

Connect on the Facebook Group

Feel free to join us on the Facebook group and share your insights or post a video of yourself reading a paragraph or two of something you wrote using this journal.

VISIT AND/OR JOIN THE FACEBOOK GROUP:
Write and Create with Lisa Tener

https://www.facebook.com/groups/writeandcreatewithlisatener

Week 2: Inspiration

Things that happened this week that I could write about:

1. _____

2. _____

3. _____

4. _____

5. _____

Things that inspired me this week:

1. _____

   _____

2. _____

   _____

3. _____

   _____

4. _____

   _____

5. _____

   _____

Week 3: Planning Page

Welcome to Week 3!

Write in the day and time you plan to write. Once you complete a prompt, return here and color in the dot.

Day 15: Date _____ Time for Writing: _____ Prompt completed: ○

Day 16: Date _____ Time for Writing: _____ Prompt completed: ○

Day 17: Date _____ Time for Writing: _____ Prompt completed: ○

Day 18: Date _____ Time for Writing: _____ Prompt completed: ○

Day 19: Date _____ Time for Writing: _____ Prompt completed: ○

Day 20: Date _____ Time for Writing: _____ Prompt completed: ○

Day 21: Date _____ Time for Writing: _____ Prompt completed: ○

Plan for at least 8 minutes to make your list, do the journaling exercise, and, optionally, scan/watch the short video (or listen to the audio meditation). If you're on a roll, by all means write for as long as you want.

Day 15

Enhance Your Writing Space for Creativity and Flow

In this video, Sherry Burton (Ways) Steine, author of *Feel Good Spaces,* speaks from her feel-good writing space, and reveals three ways to enhance a writing space to invite inspiration and flow:

WATCH THE VIDEO:

Enhance Your Writing Space for Creativity and Flow

https://www.lisatener.com/3-ways-to-enhance-your-writing-space-for-creativity-and-flow/

I tend to write in nature, in bed in the morning, or at my desk. In both my bedroom and office, I've hung watercolor paintings my mom painted. One of her most inspiring paintings—that of a beach, a wave, the pink-blushed sky, and the masterful play of light on the water—hangs just above my computer and I often rely on it for inspiration. In fact, I just looked at it now to bring my writing to life.

Five ways I can spruce up my writing space to spark increased creativity and flow:

1. _____

2. _____

3. _____

4. _____

5. _____

Pick one and write about how and why that inspires you and how you might implement it. Or write about more than one if you want. Then do it!

_____

_____

_____

_____

_____

_____

_____

_____

_____

_____

_____

_____

_____

_____

_____

_____

_____

_____

_____

"[Your writing] space should have a function, flow, and a feel to it."

— Sherry Burton (Ways) Steine, author of *Feel Good Spaces*

"Before you add anything new, see what you're holding onto in your writing space and ask whether it still serves a useful purpose. Perhaps you can let go of something old before you add anything new."

— Lisa Tener

Day 16

My Dream Reader

Watch the video to hear what two Amazon reviews say about Dr. Arun Singh's multi-award-winning memoir *Your Heart, My Hands,* and Dr. Singh's response:

WATCH THE VIDEO:
My Dream Reader

https://www.lisatener.com/my-dream-reader/

In grammar school, I tutored Cathy, a second grader who couldn't read and didn't seem to want to learn. The turning point occurred when I discovered she loved to act. I came up with the idea of us acting out scenes from our book. In order for her to learn her part, however, she had to read it first. That evening, when her mother arrived to take her home, we acted out the scenes, her mother applauded wildly, and Cathy was hooked. All she needed was an audience of one! This became our ritual thereafter and Cathy became a skilled reader. I like to image people like Cathy finding similar inspiration to become a writer in *The Joy of Writing Journal.*

Five people I would love to have read my work and be moved by it:

1. _____

2. _____

3. _____

4. _____

5. _____

So, imagine Oprah (or whomever you listed) reads your writing. What does she say or do? How does your writing affect the person? What does this mean to you? Describe the experience in detail.

"If one person reads your work and is moved by it, that is power. If you re-read your journal or writing and it uplifts you or provides you with insights, that is power, too."

— Lisa Tener

"In my heart of hearts, I was not at all writing for the people who already knew the information … I was not writing for those who would appreciate reading something clever. I realized I was writing for all the people for whom these would be *new words,* those who could benefit from those words."

— Kevin Bader, author of *New Words*

Day 17
Cozy Up

This video shows what creates coziness for several writers I know:

WATCH THE VIDEO:

Cozy Up

https://www.lisatener.com/cozy-up/

Despite the papers piled beside me and the empty bowl from breakfast on my desk, my office feels cozy to me: my mom's painting of the ocean hangs above my computer; our Labradoodle, Sophie, is curled in a tight circle and napping in her L.L. Bean day bed; and the pink flowering mandevilla vine blooms outside my office window.

How about you?

Ten things that feel cozy to you:

1. _____
2. _____
3. _____
4. _____
5. _____
6. _____
7. _____
8. _____
9. _____
10. _____

Pick one or more and start or end a story with that bit of coziness. Or write a free form poem about your list, or one item from the list.

"My perfect cozy setting to journal in includes a big fuzzy blanket in front
of the fireplace and a steaming hot cup of cinnamon tea."

— Megan Gunnell, LMSW, Founder of Thriving Well Institute

"In the marrow of winter, I go to bed with bulky, organic wool socks on my feet, a wool sweater over my PJs, and a cashmere knit cap. My husband calls this my 'birth control' outfit but it sure feels cozy to me."
— Lisa Tener

Day 18

Inviting in Life's Magic

Watch the video for a story of a special—and highly unexpected—connection to nature, and how it came about the other day:

WATCH THE VIDEO:
Inviting In Life's Magic

https://www.lisatener.com/inviting-in-lifes-magic/

Yesterday, on my way home from an herbal workshop on Watson Farm, I passed two teen boys, friends of my son, in baby blue zip-up unicorn costumes replete with rainbow-colored horns. A minute later, my neighbor, Barbara, invited me and my family to join an impromptu greeting party to congratulate Erin and Max, a pair of just-wed neighbors, as the wedding party processioned from beach to home. When the happy couple rose over the hill and we threw our rose petals, rice, or bird seed (whatever we could find), their joy was obvious.

I loved the herbal workshop I attended on the farm, but it could not match the unpredictable events of the day: the teenaged unicorns and the witnessing of a loving community out to celebrate a sacred union. Often, the most fulfilling experiences are unplanned. Such surprises require making space in the day for them to show up—taking a break from work, walking outdoors, slowing down.

Five surprising or miraculous things that could happen today:

1. _____

2. _____

3. _____

4. _____

5. _____

Pick one or more of these possibilities. Explore, imagine, have fun with it. Describe it in detail.

_____

_____

_____

_____

_____

_____

_____

_____

_____

_____

_____

_____

_____

_____

_____

_____

_____

_____

"I meditate, do a few journal prompts, and drink my coffee. This triple-step ritual bookends my day."

— Kristin Meekhof, author of *A Widow's Guide to Healing*

"Nothing chases *qi* away more easily than tension.
Soften. Soften. Soften."

— Leah Franklin, Mei Hua Qigong Master

Day 19
Move and Flow

Watch the video to see Laurie Hunt, founder of the *More-in-Me MOVEment*, describe how movement benefits her writing:

WATCH THE VIDEO:
How Movement Benefits Writing

https://www.lisatener.com/how-movement-benefits-writing/

My favorite tool for generating creative flow is to precede my writing or journaling practice by walking, dancing, yoga, or qigong movements. When I get moving, my creativity flows.

Name five ways of moving that elevate your mood and generate a state of flow:

1. _____
2. _____
3. _____
4. _____
5. _____

Pick one and write about a particular experience doing that activity and the way it made you feel. Or write about the activity as if you are doing it now, using the present tense.

"Journaling allowed me to be myself with myself."

— Martha Rhodes, *3,000 Pulses Later*

"My skin tingles as I step into the music, give in to the icy thrill of pleasure that spreads through me whenever I dance, the pleasure of leaping into a cool lake on a sweltering day."
— Padma Venkatraman, *A Time to Dance*

Day 20
Words We Love

In this fun video, authors share their favorite words:

WATCH THE VIDEO:
Words We Love

https://www.lisatener.com/words-we-love/

Certain words evoke particular emotions, a felt experience of their meaning. Some words I love: numinous, luminous, buoyant, yearn, revel, swirl, restore, awe, joy, smile.

List ten of your favorite words:

1. _____
2. _____
3. _____
4. _____
5. _____
6. _____
7. _____
8. _____
9. _____
10. _____

Pick one to start your writing and one to end it. Extra credit if any of the other words make it into your writing as well.

"Words are, of course, the most powerful drug used by mankind."

— Rudyard Kipling, short story writer, poet, and novelist

"You have more ways than ever to share your words to make a difference."

— Michael Larsen, *Writing Success Guaranteed: How to Deal Yourself Five Hearts to Build a Career*

Day 21
How I Got Screwed Out of Inner Peace

Watch the video for three tales of self-improvement routines gone awry:

WATCH THE VIDEO:

How I Got Screwed Out of Inner Peace

https://www.lisatener.com/how-i-got-screwed-out-of-inner-peace/

My husband once joked about writing a book called *How I Got Screwed Out of Inner Peace.* We laughed at the irony of the title: it captures the ways we fail to take responsibility for our own peace or work so hard at improving ourselves that peace escapes us. As a former—and sometimes current—self-help junkie, who is always trying to become the new and improved version of me, I find personal growth can support us on our spiritual path, but it can also take us in circles when we try to reach an impossible destination and never accept the beauty of who we are.

Ten ways I try to grow or improve myself:

1. _____

2. _____

3. _____

4. _____

5. _____

6. _____

7. _____

8. _____

9. _____

10. _____

Pick one of your self-help methods and write about it. Choose the hardest thing. Or the most ridiculous one. Or the one that most inspires you in the moment. Or write about them all! In what ways has self-improvement supported you? In what ways has it become a trap? Do you over do it? Are you cheating yourself out of inner peace by taking on too much?

"I tried my hardest to transform myself into a machine like him overnight."

— Adam Jablin, *Lotsaholic*

"The more you stress about perfection, the more likely you are to lose your shit."
— Carla Naumburg, PhD, *How to Stop Losing Your Sh*t with Your Kids*

Week 3: Summary

How does it feel to be writing for three weeks? I hope you're proud of this accomplishment.

Connect on the Facebook Group

Here's another invitation to join us in the Facebook group and share your insights or post a video of yourself reading a paragraph or two of something you wrote using this journal.

VISIT AND/OR JOIN THE FACEBOOK GROUP:
Write and Create with Lisa Tener

https://www.facebook.com/groups/writeandcreatewithlisatener

Week 3: Inspiration

Things that happened this week that I could write about:

1. _____

2. _____

3. _____

4. _____

5. _____

Things that inspired me this week:

1. _____

_____

2. _____

_____

3. _____

_____

4. _____

_____

5. _____

_____

Week 4: Planning Page

Welcome to Week 4!

Write in the day and time you plan to write. Once you complete a prompt, return here and color in the dot.

Day 22: Date _____ Time for Writing: _____ Prompt completed: ◯

Day 23: Date _____ Time for Writing: _____ Prompt completed: ◯

Day 24: Date _____ Time for Writing: _____ Prompt completed: ◯

Day 25: Date _____ Time for Writing: _____ Prompt completed: ◯

Day 26: Date _____ Time for Writing: _____ Prompt completed: ◯

Day 27: Date _____ Time for Writing: _____ Prompt completed: ◯

Day 28: Date _____ Time for Writing: _____ Prompt completed: ◯

Plan for at least 8 minutes to make your list, do the journaling exercise, and, optionally, scan/watch the short video (or listen to the audio meditation). If you're on a roll, by all means write for as long as you want.

Day 22
Perfectly Flawed

Watch this video of my author friends sharing a flaw and its flipside:

WATCH THE VIDEO:
Perfectly Flawed

https://www.lisatener.com/video-perfectly-flawed/

My flaws: I can be a terrible listener, even talking over my husband or kids at times. I have a tendency to rush, to take too much on. I forget to breathe. Well, not completely, obviously. But I can get tense and anxious and forget to take care of myself: mind, body, and soul. These flaws have also led me to some of my most profound experiences: learning to breathe fully and deeply in qigong class, and discovering the power of the breath for centering and creative flow, for example.

How about you?

Share five flaws or strengths of yours (or someone you admire):

1. _____

2. _____

3. _____

4. _____

5. _____

Pick one and explore both sides of the coin—ways the strength is also a flaw, how the flaw is also a strength, or how the flaw led you to a deeper exploration or new skill.

This exercise can help in developing your story's characters, particular when writing narrative fiction or nonfiction. Three-dimensional, complex characters make for good reading. Every hero has an Achilles heel (or two) and every villain has a soft spot.

"It is painful to be dependent on perfect outcomes."

— Dr. Carrie Barron, *The Creativity Cure*

"Read a thousand books, and your words will flow like a river."

— Lisa See, *Snow Flower and the Secret Fan*

Day 23

Farm to Table

In this video, Stephanie Meyers shares a reflection about her then four-year-old daughter, as she perched on a rickety ladder to pick an apple:

WATCH THE VIDEO:
Farm to Table

https://www.lisatener.com/farm-to-table/

Americans love to read and write about food. Do you? I particularly like to write about the food I grow and pick for myself and my loved ones by making my way through the prickly tangle of abundant raspberry bushes in July, or foraging for stinging nettles in the spring and summer in a far corner of a local farm where they grow around an abandoned piece of farm equipment. I feel such gratitude to the plants and all the energies that go into their growth, and for the nourishment they provide me and my family.

List ten foods you love (or hate):

1. _____

2. _____

3. _____

4. _____

5. _____

6. _____

7. _____

8. _____

9. _____

10. _____

Pick one food and imagine its journey to your table. Write in your voice or the food's voice, or the voice of someone involved in the growing/baking/cooking/preparing process. Or write anything you want about the food or make up a story about it.

"No one should have to live without gravy."

— Micaela Cook Karlsen,
A Plant-Based Life

"So, it had to be oranges. Round, sun-kissed, sweet, juicy oranges."

— Rabbi Tamara Kolton, PhD, on the title of her book,
Oranges for Eve

Day 24
An Unlikely Dialogue

Watch the video for an imagined and unlikely dialogue between two interesting characters/people:

WATCH THE VIDEO:
An Unlikely Dialogue

https://www.lisatener.com/an-unlikely-dialogue/

List five people you know who have interesting personalities:

1. _____

2. _____

3. _____

4. _____

5. _____

Pick two and imagine a conversation between them.

"Dialogue is one of the most powerful tools in a writer's toolbox because it reveals vital information about the speaker and the listener, at the same time."
— Lynne Heinzmann, author of *The Curious Childhood of Wanton Chase*

"Good dialogue is not real speech—it's the illusion of real speech."

— Ernest Hemingway, author

Day 25
Quirks as Perks

Watch the video of authors sharing the quirky personality traits and gifts that help make them strong writers:

WATCH THE VIDEO:
Quirks as Perks

https://www.lisatener.com/quirks-as-perks/

I'm amazed by the variety of gifts people bring to their writing. Some writers possess great powers of observation, especially when it comes to people and dialogue. Others have an extraordinary memory. Me? I think one of my gifts is my ability to tap into creative flow. Another? My love of the sounds and rhythm of words. Being a slow reader actually makes me a good editor: I hear each word in my head as I read.

List five gifts that help you write:

1. _____

2. _____

3. _____

4. _____

5. _____

Pick one and write about it. Or write about more than one. Celebrate your gifts. Is there a story in it?

"I have a talent I've cultivated over the years that doesn't exactly fit on a resume: I've always been a good daydreamer."

— Judy Gitenstein, author and publishing consultant

"I find the creative process of playing music is very similar to that of writing... often what emerges is unexpected and exciting!"
— Dr. Michelle Braun, author of *High-Octane Brain*

Day 26
If My House Could Talk

Watch the video for a favorite writer reading her take on this prompt:

WATCH THE VIDEO:

If My House Could Talk

https://www.lisatener.com/if-my-house-could-talk/

My living room is the perfect place to read a book or write one. Everyone hangs out there and I love when we're all reading, feet overlapping on the couch. However, we have a galley kitchen; so we also dine, stretch, and even game in the large living room. And when someone's gaming there, using his outside voice, I skedaddle.

My favorite (or least favorite) room in my house is: _____.

Imagine a bizarre or humorous thing happening in that room before you entered it and write about it. Or imagine if the room could talk; what stories would it tell? This prompt will help you develop the skill of compelling plot development. Not writing a narrative? That's okay. It also helps with scene setting for writing an anecdote.

"The walls have become our home, where with a single, tender gaze our eyes might slip into other spaces, other times, places where memories and fantasies linger in the shadows and lines of color brought to life."
— Janice Harper, *Three Chairs to Rattle My Walls*

"Happiness is a small house, with a big kitchen."

— Alfred Hitchcock, film director,
producer, and screenwriter

Day 27

Bless Your Little Cotton Socks

Watch the video of authors sharing a phrase from their dear mom, grandma, or teacher:

WATCH THE VIDEO:

Bless Your Little Cotton Socks

https://www.lisatener.com/bless-your-little-cotton-socks/

The only times my Grandma Lily raised her voice is when we kids yelled, "Shut up!" at each other. "I hate that shut up," she'd say. We'd promptly amend our request to "Please be quiet," in the loudest, angriest tone we could muster. Grandma also spoke with a pronounced Viennese accent. We laughed many times when we recalled how she once proudly declared, "Uncle Howard says I've completely lost my accident," when she meant to say "accent." Possessing a good sense of humor, Grandma laughed along with us. Remembering specific expressions our loved ones used to say can bring them back to us in full living color.

List five things your mother/father/grandmother/grandfather often says/said:

1. _____

2. _____

3. _____

4. _____

5. _____

Pick one and start a story with that phrase. See where it takes you.

"There's a grave danger you'll live."

— Diane Radford, MD,
quoting her late mother in
Bless Your Little Cotton Socks

"Choose to love and remember. You are full. You are alive."

— Kimber Simpkins, *Full: How I Learned to Satisfy My Insatiable Hunger and Feed My Soul*

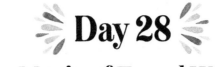

Day 28
The Magic of Travel Writing

Listen to a snippet from my journal written during a magical trip to Puerto Rico's El Dorado coast:

> **WATCH THE VIDEO:**
> The Magic of Travel Writing
>
> https://www.lisatener.com/the-magic-of-travel-writing/

      Last December, my husband planned a family vacation to the El Dorado coast in Puerto Rico. I have no idea why I felt such resistance to traveling at the time but I knew he needed this vacation so I went along for the ride on what became one of the most magical vacations our family has ever experienced. I did qigong on the beach every morning while my guys snorkeled or swam. We discovered several gorgeous hikes along the coast. A natural, relaxing rhythm replaced the hectic pace of the holidays and I returned home feeling renewed and refreshed, with a couple of completed chapters for a book I am working on.

My most exotic, thrilling, or memorable vacation spot is _____.

Write about an experience in this spot, using all your senses to describe it, and perhaps tell a story about something that happened there.

"I could read it on their faces. That foreigner is gonna get fat."

— Karin Esterhammer, *So Happiness to Meet You:*
Foolishly, Blissfully Stranded in Vietnam

"The disorientation of jet lag, foreign tongues, and unfamiliar scenery can temporarily unseat the ego and allow an expanded sense of reality to seep into consciousness, inspiring new avenues of creativity and fresh ways of experiencing the world."

— Lisa Tener

Week 4: Summary

And now you've completed four weeks of writing. Congratulations!

Connect on the Facebook Group

Once again, feel free to join us in the Facebook group and share your insights or post a video of yourself reading a paragraph or two of something you wrote using this journal.

VISIT AND/OR JOIN THE FACEBOOK GROUP:
Write and Create with Lisa Tener

https://www.facebook.com/groups/writeandcreatewithlisatener

Week 4: Inspiration

Things that happened this week that I could write about:

1. _____

   _____

2. _____

   _____

3. _____

   _____

4. _____

   _____

5. _____

   _____

Things that inspired me this week:

1. _____

   _____

2. _____

   _____

3. _____

   _____

4. _____

   _____

5. _____

   _____

Future Planning Page

Welcome to the Future!

Two more days of prompts … and more.

Write in the day and time you plan to write. Once you complete a prompt, return here and color in the dot.

Day 29: Date _____ Time for Writing: _____ Prompt completed: ○

Day 30: Date _____ Time for Writing: _____ Prompt completed: ○

Now, plan ahead for the future. Will you choose specific days of the week and times to write, and harness the power of routine? Will you find an accountability partner to help you stay the course? You can even start a writing circle to support each other to write consistently. After this week's prompts, you'll find additional suggestions. You can return here to clarify your plan.

My plan for scheduling future writing:

_____

_____

_____

_____

_____

_____

_____

_____

_____

Day 29

You Didn't Know This About Me

Watch and hear some of our favorite authors share a surprising fact about themselves:

WATCH THE VIDEO:

You Didn't Know This About Me, But...

https://www.lisatener.com/you-didnt-know-this-about-me/

By now you know that I practice qigong and I'm afraid to write—really write—about my ancestors. What don't you know about me yet?

- As a kid, I would sing to the moon.

- I was afraid of dying and being buried until my mom told me I could be buried in a crypt. Somehow that soothed my mind.

- And when I told my mom I couldn't sleep, she advised me to "think of nothing." I responded by spending hours in bed trying to imagine what nothing actually is. Turns out, thinking of nothing is not an optimal strategy to fall asleep.

List five things most people don't know about you:

1. _____

2. _____

3. _____

4. _____

5. _____

Pick one (or more) and write about it.

"I find the nights long, for I sleep but little, and think much."

— Charles Dickens, *Bleak House*

"Trust that your truths will lead you to your own unique story."
— Regina Brooks, *You Should Really Write a Book*

Day 30

How to Support Your Journaling/Writing Habit

In this video, you will find additional ideas to support and sustain your writing:

WATCH THE VIDEO:

5 Ways to Support Your Writing Habit

https://www.lisatener.com/5-ways-to-support-your-writing-habit/

Before we end this writing journey, let's put in place some support for your journaling or writing habit. I work with a writing coach to take me through my own "Meet Your Muse" exercise once or twice a month. It helps me get out of my own way when searching for answers to creative challenges. I also teach a bi-monthly remote workshop called *Get Your Writing Done* where we use my five steps for creative flow and everyone works on a piece of writing. It's the most fun I've ever had teaching a class.

What will you do to support your writing habits?

List five ways you can continue to support your journaling and writing habits:

1. _____

2. _____

3. _____

4. _____

5. _____

Write a brief plan for how you will support yourself to continue writing. Start with what your needs are: scheduling a specific time and place to write, a writing ritual, accountability, support, guidance, feedback, and community. Consider what would best meet each of those needs and your budget: a writing course, a coach, an online writing community, working with an accountability partner, or some combination of these. Imagine yourself tomorrow, putting that plan into action from the moment you wake up. Write about embracing your plan and how the day unfolds because of this.

"Intelligent planning is not the enemy of creative genius."
— Stuart Horwitz, *Book Architecture*

"If you find yourself asking, 'Who am I to be so bold?' ask instead, 'Who am I to withhold my creative gifts?'"

— Lisa Tener

Time to Become a Prompts Maker!

Your 30-day journaling journey may be over but your lifelong journaling journey continues. In addition to returning to the lists you've made to create new material, you can also become your own prompts maker.

Some days you may just want to journal about gratitude, a challenge, or whatever comes to mind. Yet, other times, it may be helpful to have some prompts handy. Ready to become a writer of prompts and create your own storehouse of inspiration? Here we go:

 **Interview You**

Imagine interviewing yourself about personal influences, inspirations, and dreams. Below, make a list of five or more questions to ask yourself about these influences, inspirations, and/or dreams and list them here.

1. _____

_____

2. _____

_____

3. _____

_____

4. _____

_____

5. _____

_____

Now, write one question at the top of each of the following five pages. These are your new prompts! You can use them as prompts for the next five days or keep them for whenever you need one.

Question/Prompt 1:

Question/Prompt 2:

Question/Prompt 3:

Question/Prompt 4:

Question/Prompt 5:

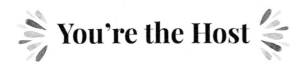 You're the Host

Imagine you're a talk show host or podcast host, interviewing someone you admire, perhaps a revered role model, writer, leader, artist, or an expert in your field.

Write the person's (or people's) name below.

Interviewee Name(s): _____

Then come up with five questions you'd like to ask them.

Below, make a list of five or more questions for that inspiriting person or people. Then, write one question at the top of each of the following five pages. These will be your prompts.

1. _____
   _____

2. _____
   _____

3. _____
   _____

4. _____
   _____

5. _____
   _____

Write one question/prompt at the top of each of the following pages. When you work with the prompt, you can answer as if you were that person (pretend you're channeling them!) or answer them as yourself. Or just get creative and do whatever you want with the prompt. No rules!

Question/Prompt 1:

Question/Prompt 2:

Question/Prompt 3:

Question/Prompt 4:

Question/Prompt 5:

Ask Your Muse

Today, you are going to ask your muse for prompts. Three is probably a good number but if your muse is on a roll, feel free to create as many as you and your muse desire! You'll scan the QR code to listen to an audio meditation/visualization. When the time comes to ask a question of your muse, ask your muse to provide a few fun writing prompts. At the end of the visualization exercise, note your prompts!

Scan the QR code below with your phone to access the audio, and ask your muse for prompts.

LISTEN TO THE MEDITATION:

Meet Your Muse

https://www.lisatener.com/meet-your-muse-4/

When you've completed this exercise, write your three, or so, prompts below:

1. _____

   _____

2. _____

   _____

3. _____

   _____

Write one prompt at the top of each of the following pages.

Prompt 1:

Prompt 2:

Prompt 3:

_____

_____

_____

_____

_____

_____

_____

_____

_____

_____

_____

_____

_____

_____

_____

_____

_____

_____

_____

_____

_____

 One Curious Cookie

Imagine you open a fortune cookie. What does the fortune say? Write three possible fortunes below.

My fortune cookie says:

Fortune #1: _____

_____

Fortune #2: _____

_____

Fortune #3: _____

_____

Now, create a question or prompt around each fortune:

Prompt #1: _____

_____

Prompt #2: _____

_____

Prompt #3: _____

_____

Write one prompt at the top of each of the following pages.

Prompt 1:

Prompt 2:

Prompt 3:

 Word Salad

Write three prompts that each use at least one of the following words: umbrella, wet, puddle, fringe, rosy, particular, funky, odd, psychedelic, speed, stillness, madness, annoying, judgmental, free.

Your three prompts that each use one or more of the words above:

1. _____

   _____

2. _____

   _____

3. _____

   _____

Now write one of the prompts at the top of each of the next three pages. Have fun writing!

Prompt 1:

Prompt 2:

Prompt 3:

 Word Salad #2

Come up with a list of 10 or so words that you can use to inspire your prompts. Don't worry too much about what words you choose—choose a few that are mood-based, a few that are quirky or specific nouns, maybe an energetic verb or two, or maybe a place.

Your words (separate them by commas):

Your three prompts that each use one or more of the words you came up with (feel free to write more than three prompts if you feel so moved):

1.

2.

3.

Now write one of the prompts at the top of each of the next three pages.

Prompt 1:

Prompt 2:

Prompt 3:

Big Thinks

Have you ever pondered deep philosophical or metaphysical questions? Wondered why there is suffering in the world? Or what life's all about? Imagine you could ask your most profound questions of God, Goddess, the Cosmic Consciousness, Spirit, Creator, Nature, or your version of the Divine.

List three or more big questions you have:

1. _____

_____

2. _____

_____

3. _____

_____

Write each of your big questions on the following pages. Pretend you're the Divine responding or just explore—whatever feels organic or interesting to you.

Question/Prompt 1:

Question/Prompt 2:

Question/Prompt 3:

 Bad Habits

Do you have any habits you wish you could break? They could be habits of thought, belief, or actions you continue to take despite knowing that they don't serve you.

Create a writing prompt about one of these habits or ask a question of the habit:

Your prompt:

_____

_____

_____

Now respond to your own prompt below.

_____

_____

_____

_____

_____

_____

_____

_____

_____

_____

_____

_____

The Good Habit

Do you have any habits you wish you could create? They could be habits of thought, belief, or actions that you think would be helpful but perhaps haven't been able to turn into a habit.

Ask a question of the habit:

Your question/prompt:

_____

_____

_____

Imagine you're the habit, answering the question. What does it have to say? Or use the question in any way you please. Really, you're the prompts maker!

_____

_____

_____

_____

_____

_____

_____

_____

_____

_____

_____

Now, you are not only a journaler and writer but an actual prompts maker. Share any of your favorite prompts in the Facebook group and encourage your fellow journalers to answer!

Share your favorite prompts in the Facebook group by scanning the QR code:

VISIT THE FACEBOOK GROUP:
Write and Create with Lisa Tener

https://www.facebook.com/groups/writeandcreatewithlisatener

If you have a chance, consider leaving a review of this book on Amazon. Reviews are an important part of the algorithm and help a book get discovered by other readers! You support authors and readers every time you leave a review

You Made It!

Congratulations! You've finished your 30 days of writing in *The Joy of Writing Journal*. Now what?

Things to Do Now

I wrote *The Joy of Writing Journal* as an easy and fun way to inspire you to write and to taste what's possible with your creativity. It would be my pleasure to help you build on that. If I may apply one more metaphor, I'd like to help you strengthen your creative muscle. Here are some suggestions of things to do now:

- If you're inspired, go back to the lists you created in this journal and find new topics to write about. You may need a blank journal for all the new material!

- Do any of your responses to the prompts in this journal inspire a longer project or idea? Explore it.

- Join my *Get Your Writing Done Program*: The title of this class says it all. On this one- or two-hour call (second hour is optional), we do simple practices to get into a state of flow and then we'll write for 30 to 40 minutes, briefly share insights, then write again. You can bring a specific project you're working on, bring your copy of *The Joy of Writing Journal,* or choose one of the new prompts I share on the call.

LEARN ABOUT MY
Get Your Writing Done Program

https://www.lisatener.com/get-your-writing-done/

One More Thing...

When writing is an act of the head alone, our writing does not reach its full potential. When we come to the writing present and embodied by engaging head, heart, body, and soul, we write our best, juiciest, most loving, and truest works. In teaching and coaching writers, and on my own path as a writer and human being, I've found breath and movement practices from several ancient spiritual traditions help us access that embodied state and open the gates to heightened creativity.

My next book, *Breathe Write Breathe,* is a culmination of my work with writers/authors and offers incredibly powerful exercises and prompts to help you open to your creative genius, which I promise you is there, within you. I also share stories from my life to help us access that numinous place from where our best writing flows.

Enjoy these two excerpts from *Breathe Write Breathe: 24 Spiritual Exercises to Spark Your Writing and Find Your Voice* (full working title).

Excerpt #1
The Juicy Introduction: Breathe and Flow, Alive with Creative Potential

Imagine this. You stand at the edge of the ocean on a June morning, water lapping at your feet. Waves crash in front of you. You breathe in deeply and smell the salty air. The spray feels charged with energy and your whole body feels vibrant and more alive, as you stand in the salt spray. You close your eyes and breathe in the warmth of the sun with every cell on the surface of your skin. You open your eyes. The sun dances on the waves and forms little rainbows as it catches the spray and refracts. The light raises you up and you feel lighter, more buoyant.

In this state, you are aware of the infinite possibilities of your life—and your writing. You experience the creative force within you as a living thing as real as your fingers and toes. This force yearns for expression. You feel called. Filled with this profound sense of aliveness, you return to your beach blanket or just plunk yourself in the warm sand. You pick up your journal and pen and write. The writing flows with such ease, you don't need to think about it. By connecting with something beyond your everyday self, you've gotten out of your own way. The writing is you and you are the writing.

This is the inner space we will explore together: Breathe. Write. Breathe. This is the source of creativity, where words flow freely and you surprise yourself.

Excerpt #2
Chapter 2: It Takes a Body

In order to write, we want to first create a state of relaxation where inspiration can flow. Warm-ups can serve this purpose. A deep breath, another, and another, and soon we are in touch with what most deeply wants to come forward—our truth, our voice, our heart's wisdom. One word appears, followed by the next and next, and what perhaps started superficially takes a deeper dive. You find yourself swimming in new territory, seeing phosphorescent plankton and sea creatures that navigate the depths with their own light.

Most of my life, I've been tentative in this body of mine—even downright neglectful. As a chest breather, I lived in my head. In my twenties, I once described my experience of myself as a head walking around with a body attached. Sure, I enjoyed moments of connection—dancing at parties, hiking in the northern California wilderness, and singing an Old English ballad my dad had taught me. Yet such full body awareness was not my norm.

My freshman year of college, I had the distinction of being the only apprentice in a Shakespeare Ensemble who was rejected four times before making the cut. I took it personally until I met the other players. It became immediately obvious why I hadn't been invited early. I was a novice among actors. My peers possessed skill and experience. That, and they fully inhabited their bodies: they moved and spoke with every fiber of their being.

As apprentices, we joined the actors in a weekly voice class, where I learned that a powerful voice is all about the breath. A breath from deep in the belly fuels a robust voice. With a chest breath, what is there to work with? This concept of breathing from the belly was new to me. I didn't know how to reach down that far, but everyone else in the circle seemed to get it. Each person's belly rounded, expanded, followed by the solar plexus, and then chest. I watched the progression of a person's breath as it filled the lungs from deep in the lobes to as high as the collarbones. Me? My body was a corset, secured by hundreds of hook and eye closures and taut ribbons, double knotted.

I did not learn to fully breathe until decades later. In Leah Franklin's introductory qigong workshop, we gently placed our hands as deep as our breath would willingly go. After a few breaths, slowly, slowly, we lowered our hands slightly, opening to a deeper breath. One by one those hook and eye closures popped open as my hands travelled down to my diaphragm and belly. By day two, I no longer wore a corset. I was free to breathe.

Knocking on the Door of Life

This next qigong practice is a warm-up staple. It gets your energy moving and stimulates the energy point on your spine, directly behind the navel, called "ming men" or "the door of life." The practice also energizes the central nervous system and stimulates the kidneys where the vital life force energy is stored. Kidney energy is associated with water and creativity—an extra bonus for those of us using qigong to prepare for writing and other creative pursuits. Follow these steps to find your "ming men":

- Stand with your feet hip-width apart, knees slightly bent.
- Turn to the right and swing your arms gently as they follow along with your torso, letting your left hand wrap around to tap the right thigh, as your right hand taps near the left buttock when the hand swings behind you.
- Turn left and swing your arms to the left, letting the left arm tap the right buttock from behind while the right arm taps the left thigh.
- Continue to swing back and forth, six times on each side.

- Now bring your hands up a little higher and let them wrap around the waist, the back hand tapping the point on the spine directly in back of your navel, repeating six times each side.

- Lastly, turn right and tap your right shoulder with your left hand, while the back of your right hand taps your left kidney.

- Turn left and tap your left shoulder with your right hand, while the back of your left hand taps your right kidney.

- Repeat six times on each side.

- Slow down and allow your arms to swing more gently with each turn, until you come to rest.

- Close your eyes, breathe deeply, and observe how you feel.

Thank You!

I am excited to share this next book with you. *Breathe Write Breathe: 24 Spiritual Exercises to Spark Your Writing and Find Your Voice* is perhaps the perfect next step on your creative path as a writer. Be among the first to hear when it is released and become eligible to receive bonus book material by signing up on this e-mailing list:

JOIN THE MAILING LIST:
Breathe. Write. Breathe.

https://www.lisatener.com/opt/breathe-book-and-tips/

Acknowledgments

There are so many wonderful people in my life to thank for helping me create this journal. I will do my best to remember you all here, but if you do not see your name, I hope you will still experience my deep gratitude.

Tama Kieves, when my inner critic bullied, yours was the gentle voice that reassured me, time and again, that I had a message people were desperate to hear. I hope I do the same for my readers here. Thank you. And thanks to Eric Maisel, who taught me how to get out of my own way and embrace my writing habit.

Joshua Home Edwards, my brother from a different mother, teaching mentor, guide, and friend, I am ever grateful you are in my life and support my purpose. Your idea to add more personal information to *The Joy of Writing Journal* made it so much richer.

To my students, thank you for trusting me with your most precious dreams and purposes.

Tamara Monosoff, ever since you introduced me to the idea of adding videos through QR codes, something's been brewing under the surface. A follow-up conversation with Tamara prompted the creation of this journal. I woke up the next day and wrote the first version of 30 writing prompts and immediately told Tamara, "You will be my publisher." Did I mention how much I love this book cover you designed?

My thanks to my PR and marketing team. Virtual Assistant Extraordinaire, Geri Lafferty, I'd have burned out years ago if not for your genius, loving support, and commitment. I thank God every day for your presence in my life. Kristin Meekhof, you have taught me more about strategy than I ever learned at MIT (no offense to MIT). Frances Caballo, thank you for introducing me to so many wonderful bloggers and podcasters, and their writing. Katie Snyder, Ann Noder, and the team at Pitch PR, I'm so glad I started working with you in September. Those TV appearances helped me own my chops as a creativity coach and authority, and preparing for those interviews motivated me to polish this book. Portland Helmich, my dear friend, thank you for your patience and brilliant ideas for TV interviews and videos; Dan Thibeault and Luke Patterson, thanks for your video magic. Seth Jacobson, I am very grateful for the new photos. Rachel Vane, you welcomed the book to my website. Tom, you support me in so many ways; thank you for helping me let go of the worry and be in the energy. And thanks to Chris Winfield, Jen Gottlieb, Brittany Sisko, and the entire community at the *Be Seen Accelerator*. I know you all will be a big part of the journey of getting this book into the world. By the time this book goes to print there will be so many more people in this community to thank, so thank you in advance!

Thank you to Lynne Heinzmann, an editor's dream of an editor. I knew you'd do this book justice—and more!

To my beta readers: Tracy Hart, Stephanie Meyers, Laurie Hunt, LiDona Wagner, Mia Potter, Gael Johnson, Amber Hanks, Melissa Sones, Gael-Sylvia Pullen, and Paula Schonewald: Thank you for your early (and later) feedback that made *The Joy of Writing Journal* better, more effective, and truer. If I forgot to mention anyone, please let me know and I will add your name in later versions.

For your help and encouragement during my inner search for the book's title, thanks to Lorraine Segal, Tama Kieves, Tamara Monosoff, Kristin Meekhof, Howard Van Es, and Alinka Rutkowska. What a process!

Thanks to those friends and mentors who helped me achieve personal growth and healing during this book-writing process: dear friend and prayer partner, Johannah Cremin; beloved friend, Virginia Swain; Qigong teacher, Leah Franklin, and the lineage of Mei Hua Qigong masters from whom she learned; dream shaman, Kari Hohne; loving guide, Linda Yael Schiller; dowser, Erina Cowan; and special friends Linda Broadhead and Seraina Wood. In my next book, I will honor many additional teachers, healers, and mentors who also have led me on my path.

To my family: Tom, Will, and Luke Patterson, and Mimi Sammis, you are the lights in my life! To Sophie, Izzy, Mochi, and Buddy, our four-legged family members, I am grateful for your comforting companionship. To the Tener and Arnold families, and the Patterson-Potters and Pattersons, please know I feel blessed by your support.

Thank you to my colleagues from Harvard Medical School's CME publishing and women in healthcare leadership courses—director Julie Silver, et al. Each of you has been an inspiration. To all my writing colleagues, I am forever grateful for your loving support, brilliant ideas, and presence in my life.

Melissa Sones, thank you for putting me up for so many successful awards … here's to the next batch. To those supporting readers, authors, bookstores, and libraries, especially Robin Kall, and to Wakefield Books and Willett Free Library who have sustained my reading habits throughout the pandemic! Big love also to supportive author friends Padma Venkatraman, Octavia Randolph, Donna Russo Morin, Jacquelyn Mitchard, Stuart Horwitz, Ginger Moran, Kelly Malone, Janice Harper, Gabriella Gafni, Michael Larsen, Leah DeCasare, and so many more. I love you all!

To Dana Newman, thanks for providing answers to my legal questions.

A special thank you to my many clients and colleagues who gave me permission to quote their wonderful words in this journal, and to the brave souls who appear in the accompanying videos.

I could probably go on thanking deserving people for another twenty pages, so for those not listed, please know you have my gratitude.

Thank you to everyone who contributed to this expanded edition, including Bryna Haynes and the amazing team at World Changers; the wonderful members of our Facebook group who tested the new prompts-generating exercises, and a special shout out to beta reader Lauri Diamantis whose scrutiny and creativity was especially helpful.

Thanks to you who have helped *The Joy of Writing Journal* reach readers. You know who you are. A few shout outs to: media coach Debra Alfarone; business strategist Jamie Palmer for seeing all the possibilities for expanding the message and reach; Mike Larsen, mentor and friend; book marketing guru Geoff Affleck; Whitney McDuff; and Deborah Louth for auspicious launch date selection and who, along with Maureen and Mary Ann, joined me wholeheartedly on the first 30-day journaling adventure!

Thanks to The Virginia Festival of the Book; Sean Murphy and 1455 Summer Festival; Stephanie Chandler, Carla King, and The Nonfiction Writers Conference; Best Ever You Women's Day Conference—Elizabeth Guarino and Kris Fuller; and to all the wonderful bloggers, podcasters, and journalists who shared this journal with their tribes and viewers.

About the Author

Photo credit: Seth Jacobson

Lisa Tener loves to write, teach, coach, and connect people to their inner muse and source of creativity. Winner of the Silver Stevie Award for Coach/Mentor of the Year, Lisa has helped many aspiring authors to joyfully publish their books. Dozens of her clients have won book awards, published with their dream publishers (from HarperCollins, Hachette, and Random House to university presses and self-publishing), and enjoyed national and international acclaim.

Lisa has been quoted in *The New York Times*, featured on ABC News, and appeared on PBS, HLN, and many national media outlets. She has served on the faculty of Harvard Medical School's women in healthcare leadership and publishing courses.

You may also find Lisa in Rhode Island, climbing the rocks around Narragansett Beach, foraging in the nearby woods, or enjoying her family of avid readers.

Visit LisaTener.com to discover the many ways Lisa and her colleagues can help you complete your writing projects, *Bring Your Book to Life®*, and explore your creativity.

A Favor

If you enjoyed *The Joy of Writing Journal,* if it sparked your creativity or brought you other benefits, please visit Lisa Tener's Amazon author page and review it:

https://www.amazon.com/Lisa-Tener/e/B002KPLZ0M

And please share your experiences with *The Joy of Writing Journal* on social media: @LisaTener on Twitter, @Lisa_Tener_Writes on Instagram, #JoyofWriting, or join the Facebook group: https://www.facebook.com/groups/writeandcreatewithlisatener.

Ideas, Notes, Doodles, and Stuff

Printed in Great Britain
by Amazon

45382619R00117